Our Global Village

The Republic of Ireland

By: Ellen M. Dolan
Illustrated by: Kathy Mitter

Milliken Publishing Company   St. Louis, Missouri

For Ian and James, who know the music. E.M.D.

Milliken Publishing Company
1100 Research Boulevard
St. Louis, MO 63132

Editors: Glenn Floyd, Lisa Shull
Managing Editor: Kathy Hilmes

ISBN 0-7877-0001-0

A Multicultural Experience

Our Global Village hopes to share ideas, hands—on activities, and resources from other cultures which will lead you, your students, and their families in different experiences. Learning how others live, think, and react is becoming increasingly important. The earth is a global village, and each of us is quickly affected by events, styles, disasters, and ideas from far away. Old barriers of mountains and oceans are disappearing because of fax machines and airplanes. It is important to help young children learn about and value the diversity in the world around them. Fortunate is the child who has the opportunity to interact with people who speak different languages, who eat different foods, and whose skins are different colors. This child will come to appreciate the fascinating differences between people in the world while learning that people are much the same. We hope this resource series will help create a multicultural community in your classroom as you learn and share different languages, customs, and celebrations.

Metric Conversions

The purpose of this page is to aid in the conversion of measurements in this book from the English system to the metric system. Note that the tables below show two types of ounces. Liquid ounces measure the volume of liquids and have therefore been converted into milliliters. Dry ounces measure weight and have been converted into grams. Because dry substances such as sugar and flour may have different densities, it is advisable to measure them according to weight rather than volume. The measurement unit of the cup has been reserved solely for liquid, or volume, conversions.

		Conversion Formulas			
when you know	**formula**	**to find**			
		when you know	**formula**	**to find**	
teaspoons	× 5	milliliters	× .20	teaspoons	
tablespoons	× 15	milliliters	× .60	tablespoons	
fluid ounces	× 29.57	milliliters	× .03	fluid ounces	
liquid cups	× 240	milliliters	× .004	liquid cups	
U.S. gallons	× 3.78	liters	× .26	U.S. gallons	
dry ounces	× 28.35	grams	× .035	dry ounces	
inches	× 2.54	centimeters	× .39	inches	
square inches	× 6.45	square centimeters	× .15	square inches	
feet	× .30	meters	× 3.28	feet	
square feet	× .09	square meters	× 10.76	square feet	
yards	× .91	meters	× 1.09	yards	
miles	× 1.61	kilometers	× .62	miles	
square miles	× 2.59	square kilometers	× .40	square miles	
Fahrenheit	$(°F - 32) \times {}^5/_9$	Celsius	$(°C \times {}^9/_5) + 32$	Fahrenheit	

Equivalent Temperatures

32°F = 0°C (water freezes)
212°F = 100°C (water boils)
350°F = 177°C
375°F = 191°C
400°F = 204°C
425°F = 218°C
450°F = 232°C

Common Cooking Conversions

½ cup = 120 milliliters
12 fluid ounces = 354.88 milliliters
1 quart (32 ounces) = 950 milliliters
½ gallon = 1.89 liters
1 Canadian gallon = 4.55 liters
8 dry ounces (½ pound) = 227 grams
16 dry ounces (1 pound) = 454 grams

Table of Contents

Ireland

NORTHERN
IRELAND

U
L
S
T
E
R

*Lough
Neagh*

*Irish
Sea*

*Atlantic
Ocean*

C O N N A C H T

Aran
Islands

**THE
REPUBLIC
OF
IRELAND**

*River
Shannon*

✦ **Dublin**

L E I N S T E R

M U N S T E R

Waterford

∧ Killarney
*Mount
Carrountoohill*

Cork

The Republic of Ireland

The earliest–known inhabitants of Ireland came from the European continent at the end of the Ice Age, about eight thousand years ago. The search for food led these early people along Europe's western coast to Scotland. From there, they crossed an ice bridge on foot or sailed over open water in primitive boats to the northeast coast of Ireland. At first, they lived a nomadic life, killing animals and catching fish for food. Gradually they learned how to plant and grow food, and they established communities.

A large number of Ireland's people continue to tend the earth today. Although it comprises only a small part of Europe, Ireland has given the world an abundance of fine literature, poetry, scholars, music, and art. The Republic of Ireland, which is independent, consists of twenty–six counties and covers 85 percent of the island. Northern Ireland, which is governed by the United Kingdom, consists of six counties. Four ancient provinces are still recognized: Ulster, Connacht, Leinster, and Munster.

Area—27,136 square miles (70,282 square kilometers)
The Republic of Ireland is approximately the same size as the state of Maine.
It measures almost 300 miles (483 kilometers) from north to south and 175 miles (282 kilometers) from east to west.

Population—3,791,000 *(estimate)*
Approximately 59 percent of the people live in the cities and the remaining 41 percent live in rural areas *(farms)*.

Major Cities
Dublin, the capital and most heavily populated city
Cork, the second largest city and near a seaport
Killarney, famous for its lakes
Waterford, port and center for Waterford crystal

Climate—Mild
Summer high temperatures: 60s
Winter low temperatures: 40s

Language—Irish, sometimes called Gaelic, is the official language of the country. It is spoken mainly in the western, southern, and part of the central regions of Ireland. English, the second language, is spoken and written throughout Ireland.

Religion—Approximately 95 percent of the Irish are Roman Catholics. Other religions represented are Anglican, Methodist, and Presbyterian.

Flag—three vertical bands.
The left band is green.
    It symbolizes the Celts and modern Catholics.
The right band is orange.
    It symbolizes the English King William of Orange and the modern Protestants.
The center band is white.
    It symbolizes the search for peace between the Catholics and the Protestants.

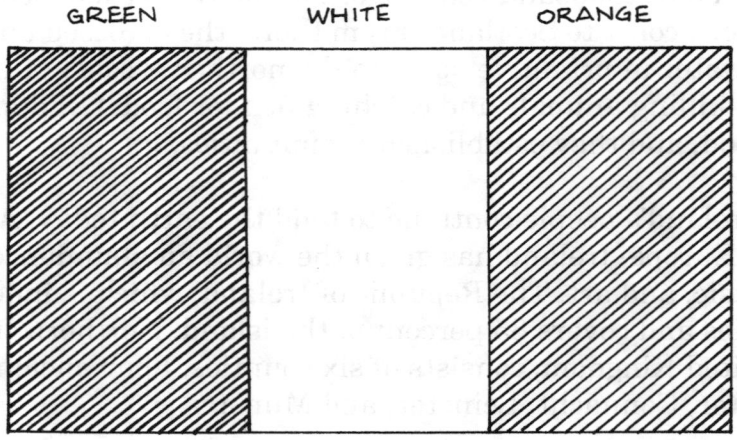

Coat of Arms—Irish harp on a shield   **National Flower**—shamrock, a type of three–leafed clover

In Your Classroom

Show the students a large map of Europe and help them to locate Ireland. Ask them to compare its size to other European countries, such as Germany, France, and so on.

Show the students a map of the United States. Locate the state of Maine, which is about the same size as Ireland. Help them draw conclusions about the differences between an island and a larger country.

Physical Features

The Republic of Ireland covers the bulk of a large island off the northwest coast of Europe. The island is a fragment that became detached from mainland Europe many centuries ago. Most of the Republic is surrounded by water. On the south, west, and northwest is the Atlantic Ocean. On the east is the Irish Sea, which lies between Ireland and Great Britain. There are many small islands off the coast. The most famous of these are the Aran Islands on the west.

On land, there are three major areas: the central plain, the mountains, and the coast. Because of the dozens of shades of green seen in the lush fields and on mist–covered mountains, Ireland is often called the "Emerald Isle."

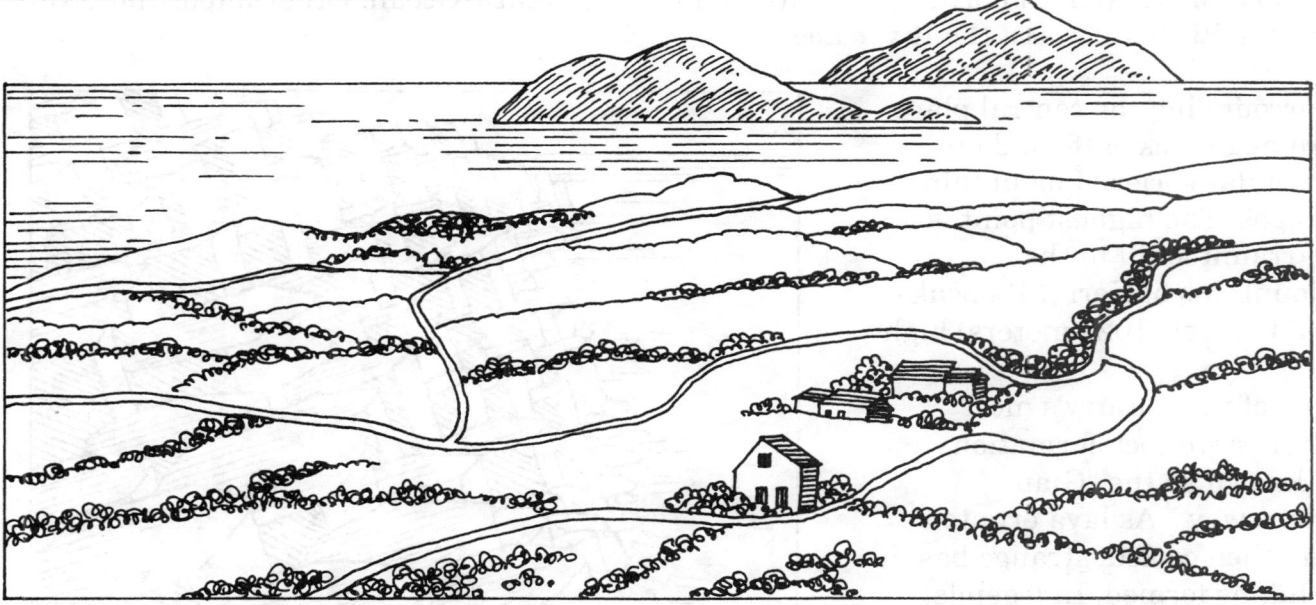

The central plain covers layers of glacial drift, limestone, and rock. This has created rich, fertile soil where wheat, barley, oats, potatoes, sugar beets, and turnips are grown. North of this are thousands of acres of wet, spongy ground that forms peat bogs. The peat, cut into bricks and dried, is an important source of fuel for Irish farmers.

Among the abundant wild and cultivated flowers on the island are primroses, gorse, heather, bluebells, daisies, foxglove, roses, peonies, iris, clematis, and delphiniums. Trees include oak, yew, beech, horse chestnut, sycamore, blackthorn *(wild plum)*, and crab apple.

While all trees are appreciated, the thorn tree is the most respected. In folklore, it is the magic tree. Trouble will most certainly follow anyone who kills or mutilates a thorn tree. In modern times, construction workers built roads around ancient thorn trees rather than dig up the trees.

After the glaciers melted, many clear, beautiful lakes and rivers remained. Lough (Lake) Neagh is the largest lake in Ireland. It covers 153 square miles (396 square kilometers). The Lakes of Killarney are famous landmarks. The River Shannon flows 230 miles (370 kilometers) from northwestern Ireland to the Atlantic Ocean. Other important rivers are the River Liffy and the River Lee.

Surrounding the central plain are huge rock cliffs and an irregular series of mountain ranges. The highest point is Carrauntoohill in the Mountains of Kerry. Its peak is 3414 feet (1024 meters) high.

One of the country's most impressive rock formations is known as the "Giants' Causeway." As lava erupted and then cooled, strange basalt columns formed. In legends, the rock formations are called stepping stones for giants as they walked along the coast and across the sea to Scotland.

Giants' Causeway

Beyond the mountains is the coastal area. It is characterized by numerous bays cut deeply into the 3500 miles (5635 kilometers) of coastline, which support the country's important fishing industry.

Animal Life

At one time, wolves, brown bears, lynx, and Irish elk—huge deer with 13–foot (3.9–meter) antlers—were among the species of Irish wildlife. Today there remain the red deer, foxes, badgers, squirrels, and hares. Domestic animals include cows, goats, chickens, and both thoroughbred and working horses. The Irish Wolfhound is the tallest dog. It has been used for hunting in Ireland for over two thousand years.

Irish Wolfhound

Numerous lovely songbirds nest in the trees and in the fields. A variety of beautiful sea birds, both native and migratory, populate the coasts.

Among Ireland's thirty–two species of fish are herring, cod, lobster, mackerel, and salmon.

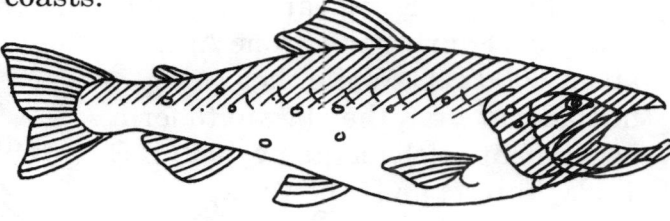

Salmon

The only reptile is the newt, a tiny lizard.

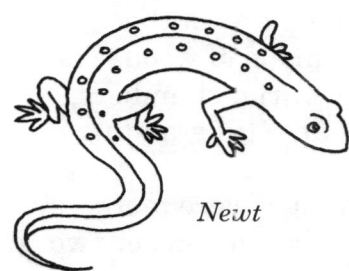

Newt

In Your Classroom

Explain that green is a significant color in Ireland. Many shades of green can be seen in the Irish countryside. On St. Patrick's Day, Irish in the United States often wear a green ribbon and green clothes to celebrate their heritage.

Ask the children to look around the schoolroom and name all green objects they see.

Have them write or name ten more objects that are green.

Point out that Ireland was part of the European continent at one time. Make a copy of the chart for each child. Ask the children to cut out the country of Ireland *(the Republic of Ireland and Northern Ireland together)* and then try to fit Ireland's coastline into the coastline of Great Britain. Explain how the underwater plates shifted, causing a part of the land to become detached.

History

Although an island, Ireland is close to mainland Europe and has experienced a number of invasions from the continent. Many of the invaders enriched Irish history and culture. Others reduced its population to poverty and starvation.

The earliest of the Irish people came from the European mainland. They lived during the Stone Age in about 6000 B.C. While they were nomadic at first, they began to form permanent settlements by 4000 B.C. Tools, knives, and other weapons were made from nearby supplies of stone. The area was heavily forested at this time, and many of the dwellings were made of wood. They also built stone burial chambers, many of which are still standing.

Mesolithic huts

Most of these tombs were more impressive than the homes. Passage graves are the simplest tombs, having one or two chambers. A corridor lined with heavy stones leads to a central chamber. Ornaments discovered in the chambers indicate a belief in after-life. Intricate spirals, triangles, zigzag lines, and representations of the sun are carved on the walls.

Dolmen—stone tables—or portal tombs have a large chamber formed by five or six huge vertical stones with an enormous sloping stone roof. Early natives thought the dolmens were burial sites of the giants. Gallery graves are similar to passage graves but are more elongated and have no corridor.

Dolmen

During the Bronze Age in about 2000 B.C., the Irish made stronger weapons than they had before by creating them from the local supply of hard bronze metal. Farming and building methods improved. The Irish built many "hill forts" for protection. Their sacrifices and early religious celebrations were held within large circles of stone. **Menhirs**, or long stones, served as tombstones and were the predecessors of the Christian high crosses.

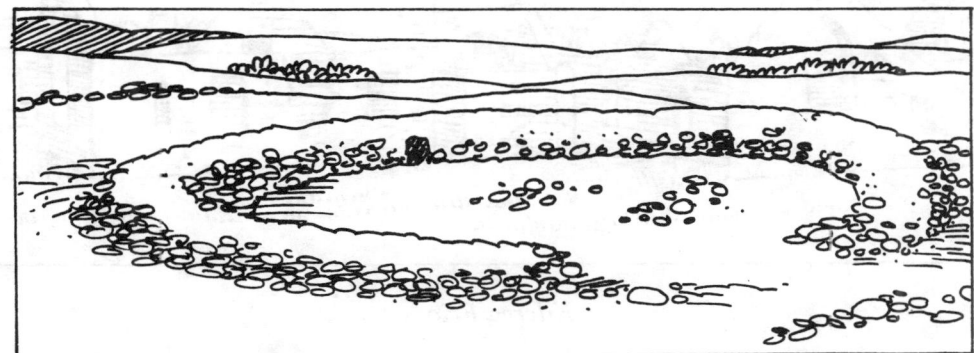

Stone enclosure

The Iron Age began in Ireland in about 400 B.C., when the Celts of western Europe invaded the island. They brought iron weapons, stronger than the local bronze weapons, and they subdued Irish inhabitants. The Celts were well–organized. They divided the country into small kingdoms, each ruled by a minor chief or king. A high king created laws, encouraged music, and built roads. The Celts had no written language, so storytellers were highly respected. Although little is known of burial customs in this age, ring forts were the characteristic fortification. Farms and huts were enclosed by a high circular rampart. Some had underground passageways that connected the dwellings. They were used to store supplies and provide refuge.

St. Patrick

In the fifth century A.D., St. Patrick, a priest and former slave, brought Christianity to Ireland. He established monasteries and taught the people to read. The monks developed a written language. While most of Europe was suffering a decline in culture during the Dark Ages, literature, learning, and art were thriving in Ireland. The famous illuminated manuscript, the *Book of Kells,* and the Celtic crosses were created during this era.

High cross

Kilcrea Friary

At the end of the eighth century A.D., many Vikings, fierce fighters and good sailors, left their overcrowded Scandinavian homeland and began invasions of Ireland. The Vikings killed people and destroyed farms, stole valuable manuscripts from monasteries, and built strong forts, which became the sites for major cities like Dublin and Cork.

Of all of the lands in western Europe, Ireland was the only one to escape an invasion by the Romans, who generally set up a system of central government.

So, although the Irish had many minor kings, there was no single leader. Then, in 1002, Brian Boru unified the country and became the high king. In 1014, Brian Boru's army defeated the Vikings and ended their rule. For 150 years, there was peace and prosperity in Ireland.

Brian Boru, high king of Ireland

Then several small Irish kingdoms began fighting each other. In the 1160s, one of the kings, Dermot, asked Norman–born King Henry II of England to help him get control of Ireland. Henry offered his Norman soldiers to Dermot in return for a share of the conquered land. Dermot led a successful invasion, but he died in 1170. After Henry II visited these new lands in 1171, the Norman soldiers declared him Lord of Ireland. Gradually the new lord's territory began to shrink as Normans intermarried with Irish and built homes. English territory finally became only a few miles around the city of Dublin. It was known as the Pale.

Later, Henry VIII, his daughter Mary, and then Elizabeth I continued to send armies and English settlers. The Irish lost battle after battle and, by 1700, were reduced to slavery. The Irish, who had once owned 95 percent of the land, now had only 5 percent. They could not vote, own property, hold public office, or become teachers or lawyers. "Hedge schools," secret spots where Irish could teach children, became common. For the millions of Irish who had no land, no food, and no political power, survival was a daily struggle.

Then, in 1845, the potato crop was destroyed by a blight *(plant disease)*. About 750,000 Irish starved to death and hundreds of thousands emigrated to other countries. Within five years, the Irish population decreased from eight million to five million. Although most of the Irish sailed for America, others emigrated to Canada, South America, Australia, the West Indies, New Zealand, Nova Scotia, and Britain. At Ellis Island in 1992, a life–size bronze statue of Annie Moore, a 15–year–old girl from County Cork, was dedicated. In 1892, Annie brought her two young brothers across the ocean on the *S.S. Nevada* to join their parents in New York. She was the first immigrant to go through the Ellis Island facility.

In 1858, a new drive for freedom began. Basically, the Irish Catholics wanted to be free from England. The Protestants preferred to stay under English rule. In the 1870s, a movement called Home Rule began. Although a bill was enacted in 1914, it was suspended until the end of World War I. Frustration over the delay in Home Rule led to the 1916 Easter Rising. After several meetings, confrontations, and compromises, a settlement was reached. The British Parliament passed a law to divide the country. The larger area became the Irish Free State in 1921. In 1948, the Free State voted to end its association with England and, in 1949, became the Republic of Ireland.

In Your Classroom

Ask the students to examine the tent structure of early Ireland and compare it to an early Native American home. Discuss similarities such as weapons, lifestyle, and so on.

Compare the writings on Celtic crosses to Egyptian hieroglyphics.

Discuss the "Dark Ages" in European history. Point out the artistic and literary achievements in Ireland while the rest of Europe suffered intellectual and cultural decline.

High cross   *Cross of the Scriptures*

Daily Life

The daily life of a family living on an Irish farm is familiar and unhurried. The same pattern has been followed for years and much of the work is determined by the seasons. Two–thirds of Ireland is farmland. Fields are plowed and planted, cows are milked, and the livestock is fed. Housewives cook, churn butter, and care for the children. Many rural families live in small stone or clay cottages, heated by peat or turf fires. Some roofs are still thatched with hay. Families enjoy each other and make room for grandparents or other relatives.

Life in the cities is similar to life in other European metropolitan areas. Some people in Ireland own their homes, while many others live in apartments. Regular office hours are kept and office workers, clerks, and salespeople ride buses or walk to work. On the way to their offices, they might stop to admire the work of a sidewalk artist or buy a piece of fruit at an outdoor produce stand. Fresh fish is also available at outdoor stands. It was in Dublin that Molly Malone, the subject of the ballad *"Cockles and Mussels,"* sold her fish. A life–size statue of Molly and her barrow stands in Grafton Street in Dublin.

Molly Malone

School is mandatory for children from 6 to 15 years old. Irish students attend primary schools similar to grade school in the United States. They study reading, writing, math, music, art, and crafts. When they are 12 years old, Irish students attend the second level of school, which is similar to high school in the United States. They can either take a course of general studies or they can learn specific skills to help them become workers in certain industries, such as manufacturing.

In Your Classroom

Point out how Irish farmers use materials at hand to build their homes. Help the students list items like rock, hay, and so on, which are used by the farmers.

Discuss the differences between Irish and American school systems.

Ask the students what subjects they might wish to add to the American curriculum.

Help the children learn *"Cockles and Mussels."* Let them take turns selling "fish" or "oysters" to students.

> *Cockles and Mussels*
> *In Dublin's fair city,*
> *Where the girls are so pretty,*
> *I first set my eyes on sweet Molly Malone,*
> *As she wheeled her wheelbarrow*
> *Through streets broad and narrow,*
> *Crying cockles and mussels alive, alive, oh!*
>
> Chorus   *Alive, alive, oh! Alive, alive, oh!*
> *Crying cockles and mussels, alive, alive, oh!*

II
She was a fishmonger
But sure twas' no wonder,
For so were her father and mother before;
And they both wheeled their barrow,
Through streets broad and narrow,
Crying cockles and mussels, alive, alive, oh!

Chorus

III
She died of a fever
And no one could save her,
And that was the end of sweet Molly Malone
But her ghosts wheel her barrow
Through streets broad and narrow,
Crying cockles and mussels, alive, alive oh!

Chorus

Language and Expressions

Irish is a Celtic language first used by early scholars. It is closely related to the Scottish, Gaelic, and Manx languages. Irish, which sounds quite different from English, is spoken mainly in the west of Ireland.

Roman	Irish	Roman	Irish	Roman	Irish
a		g		o	
b		h		p	
c		i		r	
d		l		s	
e		m		t	
f		n		u	

In Your Classroom

Ask the students to circle the Irish letters that are different from English ones.

Have the students name the English letters that do not have a corresponding Irish letter—j,k,q,v,w,x,y,z.

Ask the students to write their first or last name using Irish letters.

Rebus

Fill in the blanks with the correct Irish word.

	English	**Irish**		**English**	**Irish**
	bread	aran (g´ra:n)		dish	mias (m´iəs)
	egg	ubh (ov)		girl	cailin (ka´l´iin´)
	milk	bainne (ban´i)		table	bord (bu:rd)

1. The ⬚_____ wanted to bake some brown ⬚_____ .

2. She put an ⬚_____ and ⬚_____ in a ⬚_____ .

3. When the ⬚_____ was done, the ⬚_____ put it on the ⬚_____ .

4. She sat down at the ⬚_____ and had ⬚_____ , jam, and tea.

	English	Irish		English	Irish
🚲	bicycle	rothar (rohər)	👦	boy	garsun (gar suin)
	field	pairc (pa:rk´)	🐰	rabbit	coinin (kín´iin)
	road	bothar (bo:hər)	🏫	school	scoil (sgol)
👞	shoe	brog (bróg)			

1. The 👦 _____ rode his 🚲 _____ to 🏫 _____ .

2. A 🐰 _____ crossed the 🛣 _____ in front of the 👦 _____ .

3. The 👦 _____ fell off the 🚲 _____ and lost a 👞 _____ .

4. The 🐰 _____ ran away through a 🌾 _____ .

Many Irish last names begin with **Mc**, **Mac**, or **O'**. **Mc** or **Mac** means "son of" or "descendant of." **O'** means "grandson or descendant of." For example, **Mc**Donald means "son of Donald." **O'**Connor means "descendant of Connor." If your last name does not start one of these ways already, write it using **Mc**, **Mac**, or **O'**: _____ .

The people of Ireland have many descriptive everyday phrases and words. The Irish language has a number of words similar to ancient Celtic in both spelling and meaning. Among these phrases are:

"Slainte"—Here's to your good health. *(a toast)*
"Erin go bragh"—Ireland forever. *(a patriotic phrase)*
"Cead mile failte"—A hundred thousand welcomes. *(a greeting)*

In the English language are the phrases:

"It's a soft day."—raining gently
"fall of the table"—dinner scraps saved for the pets or livestock
"keening"—weeping or mourning for the dead
"pampootie"—a rawhide shoe without a heel, which is worn on the Aran Islands for
    climbing over rocks and in and out of boats
"praitie"—potato
"The top of the morning to you."—a greeting
"And the rest of the day to yourself."—the reply to the greeting
"Muckanaghederdauhaulia"—the longest geographic word

The Irish language has no words for "yes" and "no." When a question is asked, the answer contains the verb from the question.

Example:
Question: *"Is he going to town?"*
Answer: *"He is."* or *"He is not."*

Holidays and Festivals

Holidays
New Year's Day—January 1
St. Patrick's Day—March 17
Good Friday—Friday before Easter
Easter—first Sunday after the first full moon on or after March 21
Easter Monday—Monday after Easter
Bank Holiday—First Monday in June
Bank Holiday—First Monday in August
Christmas Day—December 25
St. Stephen's Day—December 26

Festivals
St. Patrick's Day Parades
The end of the harvest
Céile ("together")—Regular and impromptu gatherings, at which food is served and Irish
    dancers and musicians entertain
Feis ("fesh")—An all–day competition for step dancing and other traditional Irish arts

In Your Classroom

Discuss the St. Patrick's Day parades held in the United States. *(There were over 125 St. Patrick's Day parades in the United States in 1993.)*

The shamrock is closely associated with St. Patrick, who used its three leaves on one stem to teach about the Trinity. If available, bring shamrock plants to the classroom and let the students examine them.

A nineteenth–century view of St. Patrick's Cathedral

Foods

In the years after the great famines of the 1840s, Irish people ate very simple foods and were careful to waste nothing. Potatoes and bread continue to be staples in the daily diet. As the population prospered, more variety in foods was introduced. Much of it was grown on family farms. In general, Irish meals are simple, nourishing, and plentiful. However, on special occasions, Irish food can be as elegant as French cuisine.

Breakfast foods

Stir–about—a porridge made from oat or corn meal stirred into boiling water or milk
Eggs—fried or boiled
Irish soda bread
Griddle cakes
Sausage
Buttermilk
Honey

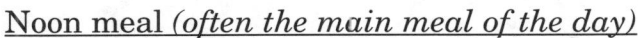

Noon meal *(often the main meal of the day)*

Soup—nettle, onion, or other
Irish stew, mutton, or lamb
Potatoes—boiled, mashed, or baked
Vegetables from the fields—carrots, onions, cabbage
Apple cake—made from fruit stored in special "apple houses"

Supper or "Tea"

Sandwich or cold plate
Cold salmon or fish

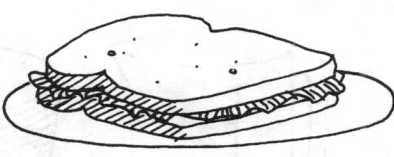

High tea *(flexible time, generally late afternoon)*

Jam and scones *(quick bread or small pastries like biscuits)*
Blueberry tarts
Cheese
Herring
Crab cakes
Fruit cake

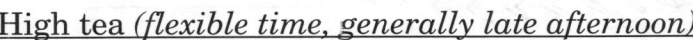

Tea is served at all meals. The kettle is always ready to heat when visitors call. The Irish brew strong tea and add sugar, honey, or cream. Traveling tea vans with many kinds of tea visit the country cottages to let people select their favorite blend.

In Your Classroom

Baked Potatoes

Wash and scrub one baking potato for every two students. Bake in an oven at 375° Fahrenheit (191° Celsius) for 45 minutes or until the potato is soft. While the potatoes are baking, help the students assemble various toppings, such as margarine, parsley, onion flakes, shredded cheese, chives, salt, and pepper. Slice the cooked potatoes in two and serve a half to each student. Let the students add their favorite toppings.

Irish Soda Bread

Preheat the oven to 375° Fahrenheit (191° Celsius). Put 2 cups of sifted white flour, 3/4 teaspoon (3 3/4 milliliters) of baking soda, 1/2 teaspoon (2 1/2 milliliters) of salt, and 3 teaspoons (15 milliliters) of sugar into a large bowl. With a pastry blender or knife, cut 6 tablespoons (90 milliliters) of shortening into the flour mixture. Add 1 cup of regular or golden raisins and 2/3 cup of buttermilk. Knead the dough four or five times (*it should not be dry*), and shape it into a round loaf. Place in a greased pan. Slash a deep cross on the top to prevent cracking. Bake 45 to 50 minutes or until done. Bread should sound hollow when tapped. Cool the bread. Serve in wedges with orange marmalade.

Baked Custard

Beat two eggs together with 2 tablespoons (30 milliliters) of sugar. Scald 2 1/2 cups of milk and pour into egg mixture while beating. Pour into individual ovenproof custard cups and bake in a pan of water in 350° Fahrenheit (177° Celsius) oven until the center is firm. Remove from oven. Cool slightly. Have the students sprinkle 1 teaspoon (5 milliliters) of brown sugar on each custard. Place under broiler until sugar begins to bubble. Cool. Makes four large or six small servings.

Creative Arts

Literature

Storytelling has always been an important facet of Irish life. In its earliest days before there was a written language, storytelling was considered so vital that the Celts assigned it a god, Ogma. The storyteller, or **séanchai** (sén á ke), was expected to be a knowledgeable historian as well as a skilled speaker. A traveling séanchai was welcomed warmly and entertained in each community.

Among the earliest of literary heroes was Cuchulain, a mighty warrior and the son of a god. His deeds are thought to have influenced the development of the legends of King Arthur. Finn MacCool was the hero of epic tales which celebrated the splendors of the third century Irish kings. Myths and fairy tales are associated with every county on the island. There were **leprechauns**, fairy folk, **banshees** who foretold death, and the **pooka**, who appeared in the form of a black horse.

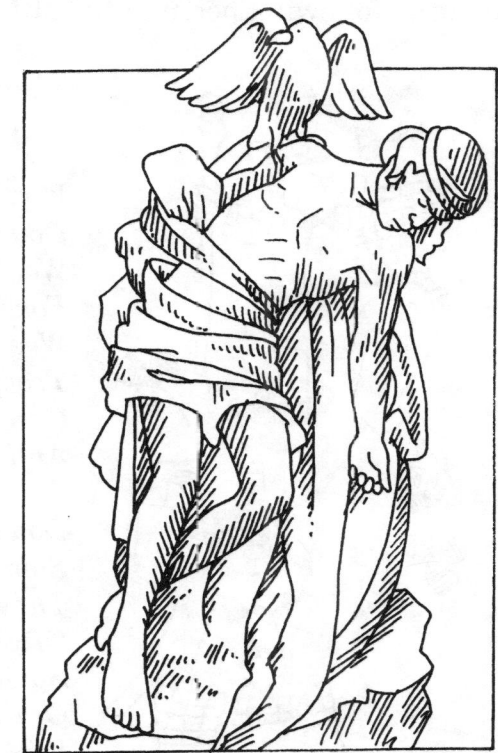

A reproduction of a statue of Cuchalain done by Oliver Sheppard

Banshee

Among the modern storytellers is William Butler Yeats, considered the finest poet of his time, who also founded Dublin's Abbey Theater with Lady Gregory. Other important Irish writers are James Joyce, Brendan Behan, Oscar Wilde, Samuel Beckett, Sean O'Casey, George Russell *(also known as "Æ")*, Liam O'Flaherty, Bram Stoker, Jonathan Swift, Padriac Colum, John Synge, George Bernard Shaw, and Frank O'Connell.

In Your Classroom

Read the following poem to the students.

The Fairies
        by William Allingham

Up the airy mountain,
Down the rushy glen,
We daren't go a–hunting
For fear of little men;
Wee folk, good folk
Trooping all together;
Green jacket, red cap
And white owl's feather

Down along the rocky shore
Some make their home,
They live on crispy pancakes
Of yellow tide–foam;
Some in the reeds
Of the black mountain lake,
With frogs for their watch–dogs,
All night awake...

By the craggy hill–side,
Through the mosses bare,
They have planted thorn–trees
For pleasure here and there.
Is any man so daring
As dig them up in spite,
He shall find their sharpest thorns
In his bed at night.

(reprise)
Up the airy mountain,...

Discussion

The little men are leprechauns, who are forever making mischief for humans. If a human catches a leprechaun, the leprechaun must show where he keeps his pot of gold.

Art and Architecture

Ireland's most famous work of art is the *Book of Kells*, a manuscript illustrated by monks about 800 A.D. The book contains Christian gospel writings, meticulously copied by Irish monks and "illuminated" by beautiful designs in glowing colors. Of special interest are the ornate capital letters in the text. Grotesque or amusing creatures were often seen in medieval art. The Kells manuscript is on display at Trinity College. Each day, a page is turned. It is frequently called the most beautiful book ever recorded.

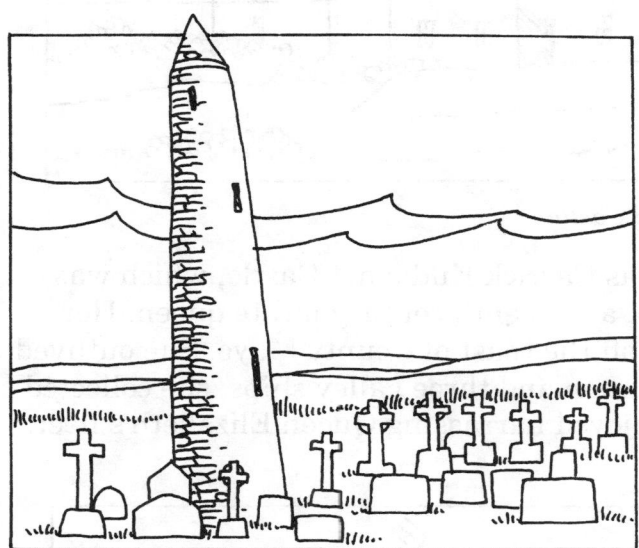
Leaning round tower

Celtic crosses, many of which are still intact, are found around the Irish countryside. They are made of stone and covered with carved symbols and figures that tell a story. The magnificent crosses are often called "storybooks in stone."

Round towers, sentinels of the past, dot the landscape. They were lookouts as well as small fortresses. The entrance to a tower was well above 12 feet (3.6 meters). It required a ladder, which could be pulled up to make the tower secure.

Castles are found on the coast as well as inland. Some are in ruins; others are still habitable. Using the plentiful stone from fields, early Irish built some giant fortresses. Later castles were built by "planters," people sent from England to settle in Ireland.

Kylemore Abbey Castle

Dromoland Castle

One of the most impregnable of these castles was Carrick Kildavnet Castle, which was owned by Grace O'Malley *(Gráinne Ní Mháille)*, a sixteenth century pirate queen. Her castle was strategically placed on Clare Island off the coast of County Mayo. She outlived two husbands and, with a band of two hundred men and three galley ships, she collected tolls from passing ships. For forty years, she enjoyed harrassing Queen Elizabeth's fleet.

Carrick Kildavnet Castle

Blarney Castle, a fifteenth century structure, is more accessible and draws many visitors each year. Visitors climb to the top of the tower of Blarney Castle to kiss the "blarney stone" imbedded there. Blarney's legend claims that those who kiss the stone will be fine speakers.

Two famous ancient pieces in gold and silver are the Tara Brooch and the Ardagh Chalice. Waterford crystal, blown and handcut, is still produced. Delicate Beleek china is popular around the world.

Tara Brooch   *Ardagh Chalice*   *Waterford crystal*

Knitted and woven material is produced both by hand and by loom. The popular fishermen sweaters are associated with knitters on the Aran Islands. Each family has its own stitch—moss, leaf, ivy—which helped to identify a drowned sailor.

Weaving flax into linen cloth was once a "cottage" industry, and the work was done by women in their homes. Today it is manufactured commercially by machines. Irish lace, either handmade or sewn by machine, is prized for its intricate and delicate designs.

Women spinning, reeling, and boiling yarn.

In Your Classroom

Have each student color the Celtic initial. Early colors were purple, lavender, red, and lots of gold. Older students may want to design and color their own initial. Photocopy and enlarge the letter T here or consult the *Book of Kells* for other letters.

The Celtic letter T, reproduced from the <u>Book of Kells</u>

Music and Dance

Impromptu gatherings in Irish homes and pubs nearly always lead to music. In general, Irish music and dancing is exuberant and joyful. However, many of its songs are sentimental and sad, often reflecting the ex–patriot's longing for home. Irish ballads sung by local singers have become popular in the United States.

Traditional folk dances like jigs, reels, and step dancing have complicated patterns. Young dance students must spend time practicing. Only accomplished dancers earn the right to wear the beautifully embroidered traditional dance costumes. "Fire and ice" is a phrase used to describe contrasts in Irish matters. In step dancing, the application of "fire and ice" is that the performer's head, neck, back, and arms do not move *(like ice)* and the feet move so rapidly that they are almost a blur *(like fire)*.

The Irish harp, the national symbol, is an ancient instrument, once played in the courts of the high kings. Other popular instruments are the fiddle, guitar, flute, penny whistle, accordion (cor–deen), bagpipes, and the **bodhran** (bow–rahn), which is a small drum made from goatskin.

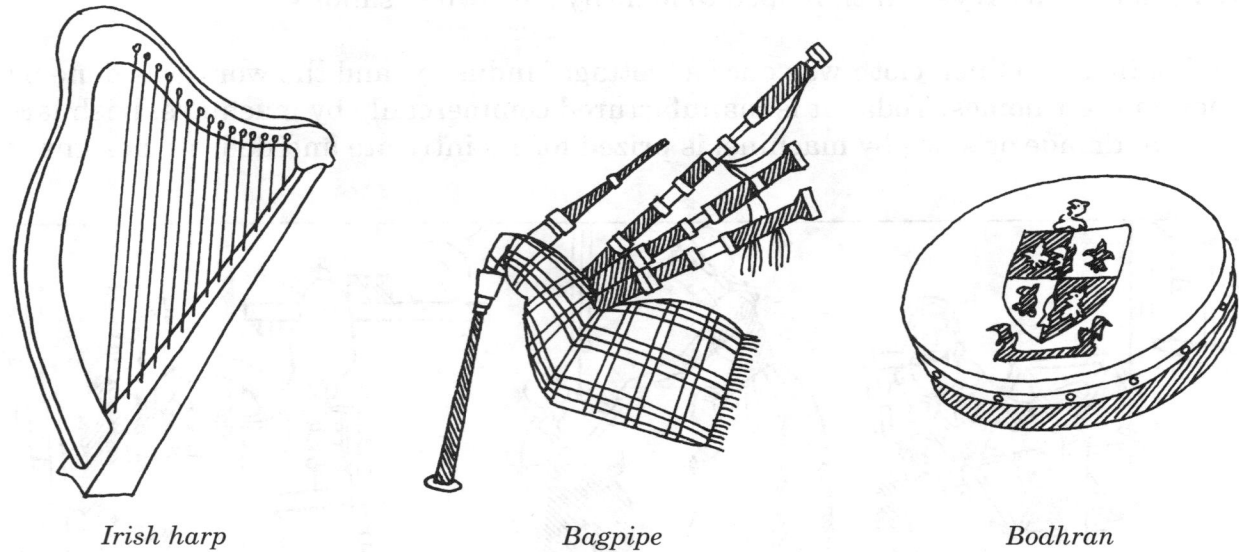

Irish harp   *Bagpipe*   *Bodhran*

John Charles Thomas was a famous Irish tenor who was exceptionally popular in the United States during the early 1900s. In the late 1900s, Irish instrumental groups such as "The Chieftains" and "U2" became equally popular. Roger Whittaker, a modern traveling musician, sings many Irish ballads.

In Your Classroom

Have the students listen to a tape of traditional Irish music. Help them to identify the different instruments.

Make miniature bodhrans by stretching muslin over clean, empty tuna or fruit cans. The bodhran usually has a symbol painted on the goatskin. Have the students draw or paint a design on the muslin.

Sports and Games

The game of **hurling**, over three thousand years old, is the most popular sport in Ireland. It is the fastest of all stick and ball games. The modern game is played by two teams on a field about the same size as a U.S. soccer field. Each of the fifteen players carry a broad, curved stick similar to a hockey stick. Players pass a small leather ball to teammates and move it toward the goal. The game lasts sixty minutes and is won by the team with the most goals. A straight shot into the goal counts for three points. A shot over the crossbar is counted as one point. A tournament, similar to the World Series of baseball in the United States, is held each year between the top teams.

Thoroughbred horse racing is also exciting and popular. The Irish National Stud is located near Dublin in an area called The Curragh. The Curragh is a large, drained bog, where the ground is ideal for raising and training champion horses. The annual Irish Derby is held nearby. There are many other racing and jumping events throughout the year.

Other sports are Gaelic football *(similar to U.S. soccer)*, road bowling, golf, fishing, boxing, sailing, and tennis. Irish children create their own simpler games. Most of these include running and/or the use of a ball.

In Your Classroom

"*The Rover*" game reflects the close bond between Irish children and the countryside. There may be any number of players. The teacher may wish to explain the meaning of "*The Rover*" before the game begins.

The Rover
The grouse and the hare
And the badger and the bear
And the bird in the old willow tree
And the pretty little rabbit
*Who lives among the cabbit**
They all have a home but ME.
(*cabbage)

1. One player is chosen as the Rover and stands in the middle of the room or play area.
2. The other players each choose a "home." An indoor home can be a chair or corner of the room, and so on. An outdoor home can be a tree, a rock, and so on.
3. The game begins as the players chant or sing "*The Rover*." When they reach the word "ME," all of the players leave their "home" and exchange it for another. During the exchange, the Rover tries to reach one of the homes. The player left without a home becomes the next Rover and the game continues.

Another ancient Irish game is road bowling. Players roll metal balls along a road or other suitable surface for 2 or 3 miles (3.2 or 4.8 kilometers). Experts can roll the ball 500 or 600 feet (150 or 180 meters) with each turn. The one who finishes with the least number of rolls is the winner. Frequently, the contest covered the road between two towns.

An adaptation of road bowling could be played in the classroom, gym, or playground. Use a tennis ball or handball, and mark off the "road" that will be used. Mark a goal line. Although teams are not a part of the original game, the students could be divided into teams for easier participation.

Additional Resources

Resources

Adams, Simon and John Breqiebec et al. *Illustrated Atlas of World History*. New York: Random House, 1992.

Book of Kells. Reproduction of the manuscripts. New York: Alfred Knopf, 1984.

Celtic Fairy Tales. Reproduction of 1892 ed. Compiled by Joseph Jacobs. New York: Dover Publishing, 1968.

Cotterell, Arthur. *Dictionary of World Mythology*. New York and London: Oxford Press, 1990.

Dillon, Myles and Donnacha O'Croinin. *Irish Dictionary*. New York: David McKay, 1976.

Early Irish Myths & Sagas. Trans. Jeffrey Gantz. Penguin Books, 1981.

Fairclough, Chris. *We Live in Ireland. Sketches of 26 Irish Men, Women, and Children*. New York: Bookwright Press, 1986.

Fitzgibbon, Constantine. *Out of the Lion's Paw. Ireland Wins Her Freedom*. New York: American Heritage, 1969.

Folktales of Ireland. Trans. Sean O'Sullivan. Chicago: University of Chicago Press, 1966.

Foster, R.F. *Modern Ireland: 1600–1972*. New York: Allen Lon (Penguin Press), 1988.

Fraden, Dennis B. *The Enchantment of the World Series.The Republic of Ireland*. Chicago: Children's Press, 1984.

Great Folk Tales of Old Ireland. Compiled by Mary McGarry. New York: Bell Publishing Co., 1978.

Jenner, Michael. *Ireland Through the Ages*. New York: Viking Penguin, 1992.

Jennett, Sean. *The West of Ireland.* New York: W.W. Norton & Co., 1980.

McCaffery, Mary A. et al. *Irish Trivia.* (Original ed.: Queenland Press) New York: Bell Publishing Co., 1990.

O'Brien, Elinor. *The Land and People of Ireland.* Philadelphia: J.B. Lippincott Co., 1953.

O'Brien, Marie and Conor Cruise O'Brien. *Ireland—A Concise History.* New York: Thames & Halloran, Inc., 1985.

O'Faolain, Eileen. *Children of the Salmon and Other Irish Folktales.* Little, Brown, & Co., 1965.

Taylor, Alice. *To School Through the Fields. An Irish Country Childhood.* New York: St. Martin's Press, 1988.

———. *Quench the Lamp.* New York: St. Martin's Press, 1990.

Wallace, Martin. *The Irish—How They Live and Work.* Praeger Publishers, Inc., 1972.

Yeats, W.B. *Irish Fairy & Folk Tales.* New York: Dorset Press, 1986.

Audio Tapes

Brady, Ciaran, Ph.D. (general ed.). *History of Ireland.* Discussion by professors. Dollanstown, Kilcock, County Meath, Republic of Ireland: Hidden Ireland Productions, Ltd. 1991 (first production).

Kane, Eileen, Ph.D. (general ed.) *Culture of Ireland.* Discussion by professors. Dollanstown, Kilcock, County Meath, Republic of Ireland: Hidden Ireland Productions, Ltd. 1991 (first production).

History of Ireland

Dawn of Irish History
Celtic Ireland
Medieval Ireland
Sixteenth Century Ireland
Seventeenth Century Ireland
Eighteenth Century Ireland
Ireland from 1760–1830
Ireland from 1782–1845
Ireland from 1846–1914
Independent Ireland
Northern Ireland

Culture of Ireland

Introduction
Language and Culture
Irish People
Literature and Drama
Irish Language
The Family
Economics

Politics
Sport
Music
Religion
Food
Philosophy
Conclusion